W9-BHO-764

Popular Dog Library

Rottweiler

George W. Braun

Published in association with T.F.H. Publications, Inc.,
the world's largest and most respected publisher of pet literature

Chelsea House Publishers
Philadelphia

CONTENTS

Popular Dog Library

Labrador Retriever
Rottweiler
German Shepherd
Golden Retriever
Poodle
Beagle
Dachshund
Cocker Spaniel
Yorkshire Terrier
Pomeranian
Shih Tzu
Chihuahua

Publisher's Note: All of the photographs in this book have been coated with FOTO-GLAZE® finish, a special lamination that imparts a new dimension of colorful gloss to the photographs.

Reinforced Library Binding & Super-Highest Quality Boards

This edition © 1995 TFH Publications, Inc., 1 TFH Plaza, Neptune City, NJ 07753. This special library bound edition is made expressly for Chelsea House Publishers, a division of Main Line Book Company.

Library of Congress Cataloging-in-Publication Data

Braun, George W.
Guide to owning a Rottweiler / by George W. Braun.
p.   cm. — (Popular dog library)
Originally published: Neptune City, N.J. : T.F.H. Publications, c1995.
Includes index.
Summary: Discusses choosing a Rotweiller, the history of the breed, puppy care, grooming, training, and more.
ISBN 0-7910-5471-3 (hc)
1. Rottweiler dog Juvenile literature.   [1. Rottweiler. 2. Dogs. 3. Pets.]
I. Title. II. Series.
SF429.R7B725 1999
636.73—dc21

99-26344
CIP

THE HISTORY OF THE ROTTWEILER

The layman is inclined to believe, owing to its name, that the Rottweiler originated in Germany and there are those who will try to tell you that it is descended from the Doberman Pinscher. Neither of these theories is fact. History tells us that, although the Rottweiler as we know the breed today is a product of Germany, the origin of the breed actually was in the ancient Roman Empire.

Behind our modern Rottweiler stands a type of short coated or bristle coated herding dogs known in ancient Rome. Today's Rottweiler bears a strong resemblance to this early ancestor; the dogs, through the ages, have shown only moderate changes in general appearance. The progenitors of the Rottweiler were reliable drover dogs, sometimes used as war dogs in battle, and we have read that the Emperor Nero always kept a number of them around his

Rottweilers are alert, beautiful dogs which have been serving mankind for about 1,500 years.

palace to discourage intruders.

The drover dogs behind the Rottweiler breed served an important function in accompanying Roman troops during their invasions of other European countries. First of all, they were needed for their proficiency at herding, for how else but "on the hoof" could food be transported for the troops in those pre-refrigeration and pre-food preservative days? A large herd for extended invasions was essential, and to guard the herd and prevent loss, so was the drover dog. These dogs probably performed other useful duties, too, on their travels across the European continent. Undoubtedly, theirs was a role of major importance in the success of these forays, due to their intelligence, stamina and powerful strength.

Through the St. Gotthard Pass over the Alps and into Southern Germany came the invaders with their dogs, into the Wurttemberg area where Rottweil is located. The city itself is the seat of the district bearing this same name; it stands on a hill on the left bank of the Neckar River, centrally located in this lush agricultural area. It is said that Rottweil was so named around the period of 700 A.D., at which farmers and cattlemen brought produce for sale. Here again, strong intelligent working dogs of stamina and good "lasting ability" were needed not only to transport the cattle, which sometimes traveled considerable distances, but for the protection of the traders themselves. On the

Two Rottweilers at play retrieving a stick. Because of their brute strength, Rottweilers have been used as working dogs, as well as guard dogs. They are a very popular breed.

the time that a Christian Church was erected where Roman baths had formerly been. During the excavation, red tiles of an earlier Roman villa were unearthed, and soon the area became known as "das Rote Wil" or "the red tile."

Some of the drover dogs and their offspring remained in this area when the troops moved on. Owing to its central location, Rottweil became an important trading center and marketplace to return journey, their moneybags were far safer tied to the collar of a formidable dog than in their own hands should thieves be encountered on these lonely trails.

The butchers, farmers, and cattle dealers came in steadily increasing numbers to the Rottweil area as its popularity as a trading center flourished and cultural interests increased. Visitors, as well as those native to the area, noticed the merits of the "butcher dogs" and the practice began to purposely breed them to improve and increase their type.

Soon a brisk trade developed with people anxious to purchase these fine animals to take home. In respect for their superiority over other types of local dogs, the might possess the best and finest dogs, and even as today an especially outstanding one in looks, temperament and working ability could bring a sizeable price. One of their attributes as herding dogs has always been their ability to work calmly and without excitement, avoiding any

Rottweilers have become very useful on farms where they quickly learn to herd and protect large farm animals like horses and cows.

Roman drover dogs were given the name "Rottweiler," to associate them forever with the area in which they had been so well accepted and appreciated. Thus it is that the descendants of the original Roman drover dogs, as the Germans bred and developed them, we now know as the Rottweiler.

Very quickly a competitive spirit was aroused among owners of these Rottweilers as to who disturbance of the cattle or disquieting behavior as they firmly keep the herd moving along together.

Another job the breed handled well was pulling a cart. Despite all their attributes, however, a time came when the new railroads and resulting regulations resulted in a different form of cattle transportation, and the job of pulling milk carts was switched to donkeys instead of the dogs, thereby depriving the Rottweiler dogs of their two principal forms of usefulness. Happily, there were some loyal owners who retained their dogs as guards for their homes and property.

A great surge of renewed interest in the breed began in Northern Germany rather than in their original "home area" (we understand that in 1905 there

opposite sex. A passing policeman who was a Rottweiler owner was out walking with his dog, came upon the scene and felt that he should take some action. Of course he immediately became the target of the mob, and the Rottweiler was the hero of the situation; in almost no time at all several of the sailors were thrown to the ground and the others were

In Europe, Rottweilers are used by the police, border patrols and the army for every kind of duty including guarding, searching, attack and camaraderie.

was only one Rottweiler bitch to be found in all of Rottweil). This took place early in the 20th century because the breed at that time had been "discovered" for police work. The amusing story we have heard of how this began has to do with a brawl one night in a waterfront saloon in Hamburg. Fourteen very drunken sailors were carrying on a dispute over the favors of a member of the

beating a hasty retreat.

It is interesting to find descriptions of the early Rottweilers as they developed in Germany prior to the 20th century. In general conformation and head shape there is said to have been little change: the massive substance, aura of power, and assured self-confidence has been present right along. A working man rather than

Rottweilers are hard-working dogs, but they are also gentle with children once they have been properly trained. Rottweilers are very intelligent but, like all dogs, MUST be trained to meet your needs.

There were two size categories of Rottweilers. The smaller strains were used for guarding, searching and camaraderie, while the larger strains were bred for attack and heavy hauling.

a dandy! Two separate strains were being developed in those days, we gather from our research: the bigger, more muscular dogs for work with the cars; the smaller, more agile and less bulky were deemed more suitable for herding. This difference was due to three considerations: the largest dogs were perhaps too heavily built for lasting stamina on the road; their extra weight might cause accidents in jumping; and their additional height could cause a tendency to nip the cattle in the shoulder or buttocks rather than on the hock as they herded

resulting in damaged stock that would bring down its value.

The two size categories were bred as separate strains. Performance alone was sought in the smaller dogs with little concern about their looks. In fact it was in this strain that the "off" coloring by present standards existed, dogs with white collars, white chests, white spots or feet, or even red dogs with black stripes down their back, or light-colored markings were known and accepted, while the larger strain was always scrupulously correct in color as we know it today.

Rottweilers are not normally aggressive and they have to be trained to attack humans. It is NOT advisable for you to attempt to train an attack Rottweiler, leave that task to the army and police where dogs are often more effective than guns.

1994 Westminister Kennel Club Best of Breed Winner Ch. Roborotts Arco Von Ilco TD owned by Martin and Florence Thomson.

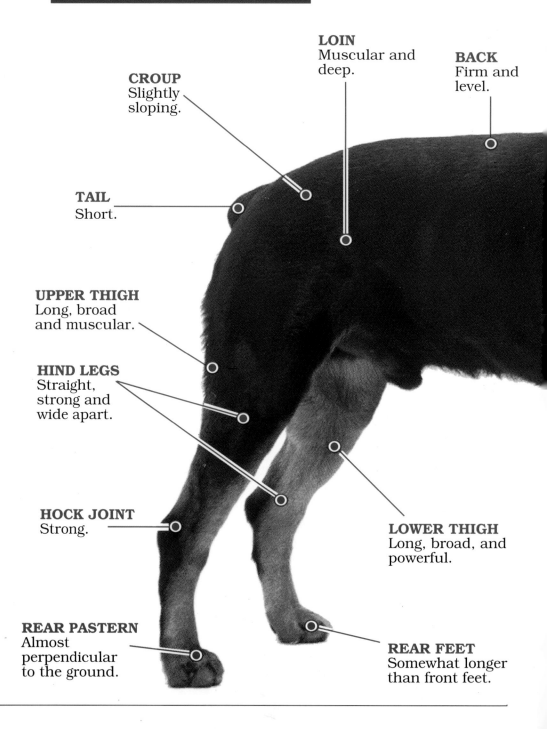

LOIN
Muscular and deep.

BACK
Firm and level.

CROUP
Slightly sloping.

TAIL
Short.

UPPER THIGH
Long, broad and muscular.

HIND LEGS
Straight, strong and wide apart.

HOCK JOINT
Strong.

LOWER THIGH
Long, broad, and powerful.

REAR PASTERN
Almost perpendicular to the ground.

REAR FEET
Somewhat longer than front feet.

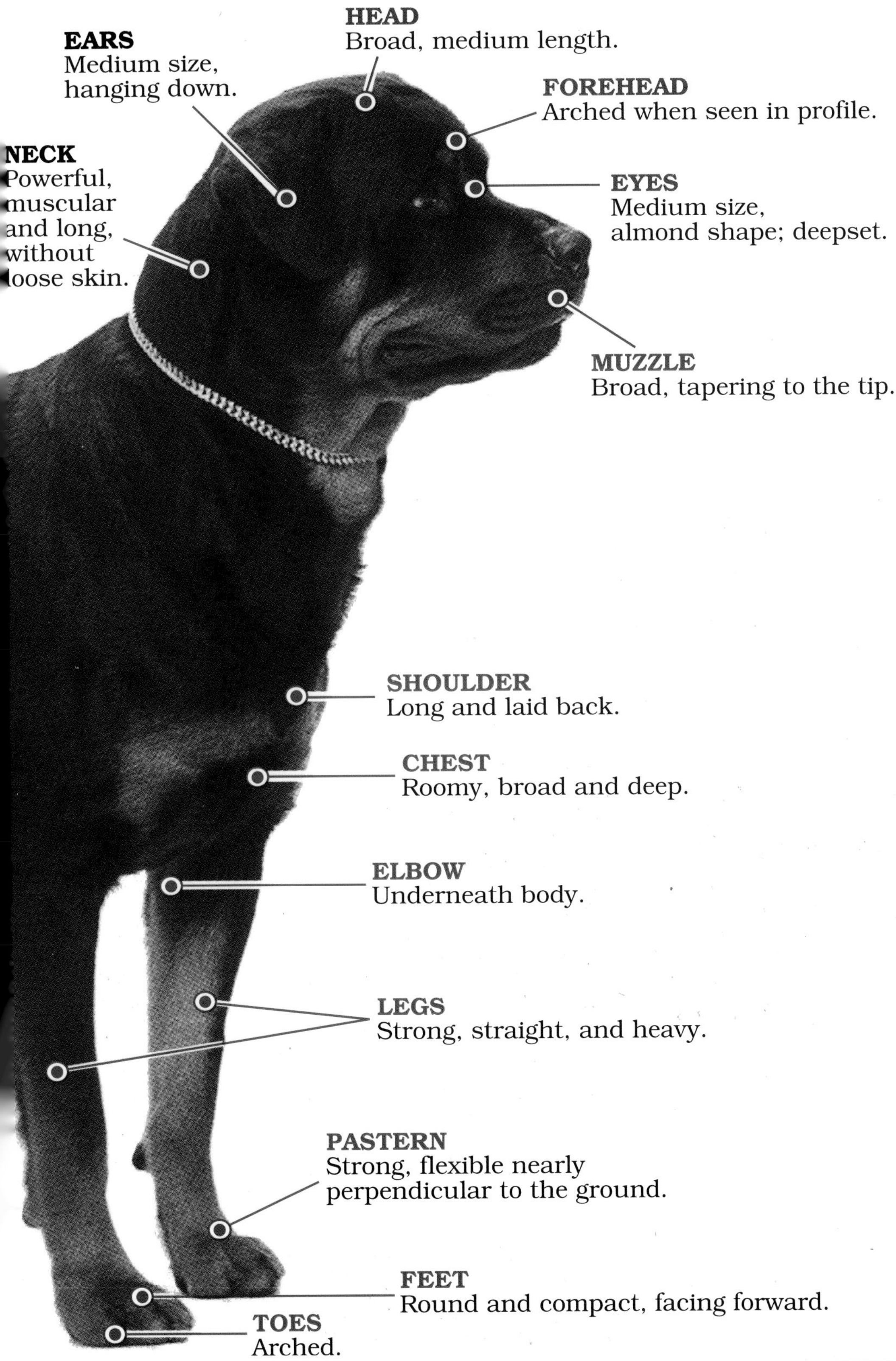

HEAD
Broad, medium length.

EARS
Medium size,
hanging down.

FOREHEAD
Arched when seen in profile.

NECK
Powerful,
muscular
and long,
without
loose skin.

EYES
Medium size,
almond shape; deepset.

MUZZLE
Broad, tapering to the tip.

SHOULDER
Long and laid back.

CHEST
Roomy, broad and deep.

ELBOW
Underneath body.

LEGS
Strong, straight, and heavy.

PASTERN
Strong, flexible nearly
perpendicular to the ground.

FEET
Round and compact, facing forward.

TOES
Arched.

The quality of a Rottweiler as a pet dog has no relationship to the individual dog's perfection according to breed standards. Unfortunately, most Rottweiler standards don't measure a dog's personality.

ROTTWEILER BREED STANDARD

A standard of perfection is the guide by which we evaluate and judge members of a specific breed of dog. Based on the accepted standard from the country of the breed's origin, these standards are drawn up by a parent club for each breed, usually by a committee of experienced authorities selected for their knowledge and willing to undertake the task. Their work next is discussed, reviewed and eventually approved by the board of directors and general membership of the specialty club, then submitted to the national kennel club for final review, examination and eventual acceptance as the standard for that breed. As the years pass, sometimes it is found desirable to review and revise or clarify a standard in order for it to better serve its purpose. That is what has happened to the original Rottweiler AKC standard, which had been in use in the United States since 1935. Although it was a good one as far as it went, it seemed to be in need of expansion to make it more in line with the original Rottweiler standards from Europe, those of the German Rottweiler club (ADRK) and the Federation Cynologique Internationale (FCI), and was thus modified to its present state. The following is an example of what a standard for the Rottweiler reads like:

General Appearance: The ideal Rottweiler is a large, robust and powerful dog, black with clearly defined rust markings. His compact build denotes great strength, agility and endurance. Males are characteristically larger, heavier boned and more

This is an ideal Rottweiler and winner of many major dog shows. It has the robust, strong look necessary for a Rottweiler.

masculine in appearance.

Size: Males, 24" to 27". Females 22" to 25". Proportion should always be considered rather than height alone. The length of the body, from the breast bone (sternum) to the rear edge of the pelvis (ischium) is slightly longer than the height of the dog at the withers; the most desirable proportion being as 10 to 9. Depth of chest should be fifty per cent of the height.

Serious Faults: Lack of proportion, undersize, oversize.

Head: Of medium length, broad between the ears; forehead line seen in profile is moderately arched. Cheekbones and stop well developed; length of muzzle should not exceed distance between stop and occiput. Skull is preferred dry; however, some wrinkling may occur when dog is alert.

A champion Rottweiler with a lovely head of medium length and broad between the ears.

This is a magnificent champion Rottweiler. Females are 21-25 inches tall while males are 24-27 inches tall.

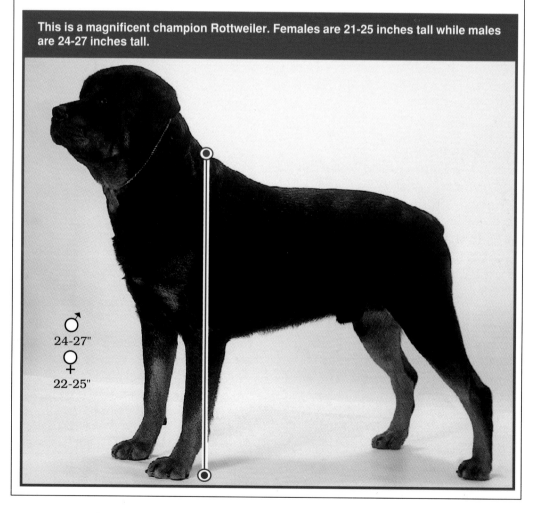

♂
24-27"
♀
22-25"

Rottweilers must always have black lips. Inner mouth must be dark. If the inner mouth is pink the dog is penalized in competition, even though it doesn't affect the dog's pet-worthiness.

Muzzle: Bridge is straight, broad at base with slight tapering towards tip. Nose is broad rather than round, with black nostrils.

Lips: Always black; corners tightly closed. Inner mouth pigment is dark. A pink mouth is to be penalized.

Teeth: 42 in number (20 upper and 22 lower); strong, correctly placed, meeting in a scissors bite, lower incisors touching inside of upper incisors.

Serious Faults: Any missing tooth, level bite.

Disqualifications: Undershot, overshot, four or more missing teeth.

Eyes: Of medium size, moderately deep set, almond shaped with well fitting lids. Iris of uniform color, from medium to dark brown, the darker shade always preferred.

Serious Faults: Yellow (bird of prey) eyes; eyes not of same color; eyes unequal in size or shape. Hairless lid.

Ears: pendant, proportionately small, triangular in shape; set well apart and placed on skull so as to make it appear broader when the dog is alert. Ear terminates at approximate mid-cheek level. Correctly held, the inner edge will lie tightly against cheek.

Neck: powerful, well muscled, moderately long with slight arch and without loose skin.

Body: Topline is firm and level, extending in straight line from withers to croup.

Brisket: Deep, reaching to elbow.

Chest: Roomy, broad with well

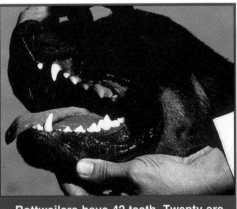

Rottweilers have 42 teeth. Twenty are in the upper jaw and 22 in the lower jaw. The teeth meet in a scissors bite.

pronounced forechest.

Ribs: Well sprung.

Loin: Short, deep and well muscled.

Croup: Broad, medium length, slightly sloping.

Tail: Normally carried in horizontal position, giving an impression of an elongation of top line. Carried slightly above horizontal when dog is excited. Some dogs are born without a tail, or a very short stub. Tail is normally docked short close to the body. The set of the tail is more important than length.

Forequarters: Shoulder blade long, well laid back at 45 degree angle. Elbows tight, well under body. Distance from withers to elbow and elbow to ground is equal.

Legs: Strongly developed with straight heavy bone. Not set closely together.

Pasterns: Strong, springy and almost perpendicular to ground.

Front Feet: Round, compact, well arched toes, turning neither in nor out. Pads thick and hard; nails short, strong and black. Dewclaws may be removed.

Hindquarters: Angulation of hindquarters balances that of forequarters.

Upper Thigh: Fairly long, broad and well muscled.

Stifle Joint: Moderately angulated.

Lower Thigh: Long, powerful, extensively muscled leading into a strong hock joint; metatarsus nearly perpendicular to ground. Viewed from rear, hind legs are straight and wide enough apart to fit in with a properly built body.

Back Feet: Somewhat longer than front feet, well arched toes turning neither in nor out.

This lovely Rottweiler conforms nicely to the standard. Its forequarters feature a long shoulder blade, well laid back at a 45° angle.

A Rottweiler having fun with a back rub in the grass. His back feet are longer than his front feet and that's the way it's supposed to be!

Dewclaws must be removed if present.

Coat: Outer coat is straight, coarse, dense, medium length, lying flat. Undercoat must be present on neck and thighs, but should not show through the outer coat. The Rottweiler should be exhibited in a natural condition without trimming, except to remove whiskers if desired.

Fault: Wavy coat.
Disqualification: Long coat.

Color: Always black with rust to mahogany markings. The borderline between black and rust should be clearly defined. The markings should be located as follows: a spot over each eye; on cheeks, as a strip around each side of the muzzle, but not on the bridge of nose; on throat; triangular mark on either side of breastbone; on forelegs from carpus downward to toes; on inside of rear legs showing down the front of stifle and broadening out in front of rear legs from hock to toes, but not completely eliminating black from back of legs; under tail. Black penciling markings on toes. The undercoat is gray or black.

Quantity and location of rust markings is important and should not exceed ten percent of body color. Insufficient or excessive markings should be penalized.

Serious Faults: Excessive markings; white markings any

Rottweilers are heavy dogs, but they are fairly agile for such a large animal. They must not be shy or easily frightened.

Above all, Rottweilers must be good with children even though this is not a criterion according to the standard.

place on dog (a few white hairs do not constitute a marking); light colored markings.

Disqualifications: Any base color other than black; total absence of markings.

Gait: The Rottweiler is a trotter. The motion is harmonious, sure, powerful and unhindered, with a strong fore-reach and a powerful rear drive. Front and rear legs are thrown neither in nor out, as the imprint of hindfeet should touch that of forefeet. In a trot, the forequarters and hindquarters are mutually coordinated while the back remains firm; as speed is increased legs will converge under body towards a center line.

Character: The Rottweiler should possess a fearless expression with a self-assured aloofness that does not lend itself to immediate and indiscriminate friendships. He has an inherent desire to protect home and family, and is an intelligent dog of extreme hardness and adaptability with a strong willingness to work. Judge shall dismiss from the ring any shy or vicious Rottweiler. *Shyness:* A dog shall be judged fundamentally shy if, refusing to stand for examination it shrinks away from the judge; if it fears an approach from the rear; if it shies at sudden or unusual noises to a marked degree. *Viciousness:* A dog that attacks or attempts to attack either the judge or the handler is definitely vicious. An aggressive or belligerent attitude towards other dogs shall not be deemed viciousness.

Faults: The foregoing is a description of the ideal Rottweiler. Any structural fault that detracts from the above-described working dog must be penalized to the extent of the deviation.

Disqualifications: Undershot, overshot, four or more missing teeth. Long coat. Any base color other than black. Total absence of markings.

Rottweilers must have a fearless expression with a self-assured aloofness. They must have an inherent desire to protect home and family.

VERSATILITY AND RESPONSIBILITY

At first glance, your new Rottweiler may seem to be just like every other cute little puppy. Big blue eyes, fuzzy face, and typical puppy clumsiness allow the young Rottie to romp along inconspicuously, blending in with all the other canine infants. However, you will see as he grows from a low-profile pup into a majestic stalwart that the Rottweiler is not just any dog. These are powerful, willful dogs who have served mankind in all types of functions for many years. When properly reared, they are excellent family dogs: loving, hard-working and reliable. They have a genuine interest in pleasing their master in every possible way. Their intelligence, sheer strength, and courage combine to create a force unmatched by any other breed. Unfortunately, these positive traits can easily be translated into negative actions should the dog's qualities be improperly channeled.

When you buy your Rottweiler his fate is in your hands. It is up to you to train him and keep him healthy.

A dog of this ability and strength needs a responsible, committed owner, one who can devote himself to allowing this talented animal to unleash his full potential. How versatile is the Rottweiler? The compact build, superior strength, agility, and intelligence of this dog make it highly trainable and very effective in a variety of roles. Like his compatriot the German Shepherd, the Rottweiler is an adaptable, super-efficient police dog, seeing full-time duty in K-9 units across the United States in addition to Germany. In wartime, they have been utilized as military dogs, guarding prisoners, sniffing out mines, and performing other diverse functions. In peacetime, the Rottweiler's strong sense of smell has been useful in drug detection and search and rescue work. Following true to its natural instincts as a cattle driver, some Rottweilers are still employed by ranchers in Germany, the US, and Australia. The Rottweiler's high intelligence and flexibility make him an ideal candidate for assistance programs, such as Seeing Eye and hearing dogs. His patience, attractiveness, and pleasant disposition have found him work as a therapy dog in hospitals and nursing homes. His protective instincts, along with a conveniently sized body, make the breed perfectly suited as a guard dog for professional establishments and homes. All these tasks and more are ably handled by the competently capable Rottweiler.

When properly socializied, Rottweiler puppies have loving and pleasant dispositions.

With all of these wonderful abilities, it is extremely important that the Rottweiler owner find the time to extract them. If a commitment is made on the owner's side, and a disciplined obedience program implemented, a special bond will form between owner and master. A Rottweiler who is left alone in a basement or tied in a backyard all day long will soon become a depressed, socially maladjusted problem dog. By nature the Rottweiler wants to be a part of the family and meaningful in the life of his master. Therefore it is necessary to give the Rottweiler a job to do, or to engage him in some kind of activity that can sufficiently vent his energy. And it is not necessary to live on a farm to make use of your dog's working abilities; a few moments of creative thinking will produce any number of tasks around the home that you can assign to your efficient companion. However, keep in mind that the Rottweiler is very bright and will become bored with simple tasks and repetition. An owner can keep his interest with variety and challenge. In addition, several clubs and organizations all over are established to help Rottie owners channel and develop their dogs' skills and talents. You can enter your dog in any of a number of sanctioned competitions, such as conformation showing, pulling meets, agility and obedience trials, tracking tests—the Rottweiler can do it all!

Such a sensible, worthy dog is worthy of a sensible keeper. Dim-witted dog owners are quickly outdone by their naturally brilliant canines. Irresponsibility on the part of the owner will result in situations of defiance and distress. In addition, it must be understood that although Rottweilers tend to be sensitive, they nonetheless require a Glove award hanging in the den, but instead an owner who indicates without hesitating to the growing puppy what is and isn't acceptable behavior. This introduction will result in a strong dog-owner bond and happiness on both sides.

Rottweilers, as a rule, are very protective of their young puppies. Don't attempt to distract a Rottweiler when she is caring for her litter.

consistent, firm hand. Obedience is not a problem with the Rottweiler if the dog has been reared properly and is treated fairly and consistently. On the other hand, if the dog is misdirected or ignored, its natural intensity, determination, and sheer strength will harden into an overly independent dog who can lose control easily. An owner with a firm hand need not be a 200-pound man with a dusty Golden With all this in mind, the Rottweiler owner has a number of options. Just because your dog is "only" a family pet does not mean he cannot partake in the various forms of exercise and work that he is instinctually suited for. There are all kinds of competitions, both for the serious and the fun-minded, that the Rottweiler owner can enter with his dog. For example, there are herding competitions that allow

Every dog requires training and Rottweilers especially require training because they are so large.

working dogs. This type of training involves three important aspects: tracking, obedience, and protection work. Schutzhund training should not be confused with attack training, as the dogs who compete in Schutzhund trials are friendly, well-behaved, controllable companions. The basic concept of Schutzhund is obedience; that the dog obey his master's commands. Because the Rottweiler has such a strong willingness to please, he is an ideal contestant in these trials.

Regardless of which path you choose to take your Rottweiler down, responsible decision-making must take place. The new

Rottweiler obediently standing during the judging at a show.

the Rottweiler to utilize his inherent droving abilities. Since the Rottweiler is also an accomplished tracking breed, there are titles to be gained in tracking competitions. Also, temperament tests are run both in the US and Germany to prove temperamental soundness in situations of varying stress and intensity.

For those interested in the aggressive qualities of the Rottie, Schutzhund is a sport that may pique your interest. Schutzhund (German for "protection dog") is a type of training that developed in Europe in the 1890s as a means for developing the full potential of owner is free to participate in various training procedures. Of course, basic obedience training is an absolute must for all dogs, and particularly in the case of the potentially destructive Rottweiler. To attain the perfect companion/guard dog, much time and dedication is required. This is true with owning any dog, but in the case of the Rottweiler, the consequences of an owner's failing to commit his all are regretfully higher due to the strength and tenacity inherent in the breed. That is not to say that the Rottweiler is nasty, unmanageable, or should be feared—this breed is not a

Minimally, Rottweilers must be trained to obey your simple commands of *SIT, HEEL, DOWN* and *COME.*

monster. However, what must be understood is that this dog, like all dogs, will be a reflection of his master. Therefore, a reckless, abusive, irresponsible owner will result in a dog that is his mirror image; likewise, a competent, caring, responsible owner will produce a pet with the same positive attributes his master teaches. The bottom line is that the Rottweiler, for all its strength, intelligence, and power, deserves an honorable owner that respects all that this extraordinary breed has to offer, and will channel these characteristics constructively and responsibly.

A young Rottweiler must look and act healthy. If you have any doubts about your Rottweiler's health, contact your veterinarian immediately.

ROTTWEILER HEALTH

Your Rottweiler is the picture of health: vibrant gold markings against a shiny black coat, clear eyes, pink gums, moist nose, and ever-alert and active. We know our pets, their moods and habits, and therefore we can recognize when our Rottweiler is experiencing an off-day. Signs of sickness can be very obvious or very subtle. As any mother can attest, diagnosing and treating an ailment requires common sense, knowing when to seek home remedies and when to visit your veterinarian.

Your veterinarian, we know, is your Rottweiler's best friend, next to you. It will pay to be choosy about your veterinarian. Talk to dog owning friends whom you respect. Visit more than one vet before you make a lifelong choice. Trust your instincts. Find a knowledgeable, compassionate vet who knows Rottweilers and likes them.

Among the most pressing health concerns of Rottweiler breeders and owners today is parvovirus. The Rottweiler breed has exhibited a stronger susceptibility to parvovirus than other breeds. Puppies should receive a vaccine every third week until they are 20 weeks old. Parvovirus attacks the bone marrow, intestinal tract and heart

Rottweilers must have a shiny, healthy coat. They must be alert and active. If they are always sitting and out of breath, the dog might be ill!

muscles in young puppies under six weeks of age. Puppies who have been vaccinated properly will show an immunity (also known as a titer) to the virus. Vaccinations must be continued until the puppy develops an immunity to this dreaded disease. Coronavirus is similar to parvovirus and also requires continuing immunization. Most breeders and veterinarians agree that a yearly booster is the safest recourse to protecting Rottweilers from parvo and related viruses. Since these viruses can potentially spread from dog to dog, immunization is vital before allowing a puppy to enter obedience or training classes.

An owner must pay special attention to the following:

Anal sacs, sometimes called anal glands, are located in the musculature of the anal ring, one on either side. Each empties into the rectum via a small duct. Occasionally their secretion becomes thickened and accumulates so you can readily feel these structures from the outside. If your Rottweiler is scooting across the floor dragging his rear quarters, or licking his rear, his anal sacs may need to be expressed. Placing pressure in and up toward the anus, while holding the tail, is the general routine. Anal sac secretions are characteristically foul-smelling,

There are many first aid treatments and observation you can make yourself. By examining your Rottweiler's eyes, ears and skin, you will learn what is abnormal when and if the time comes!

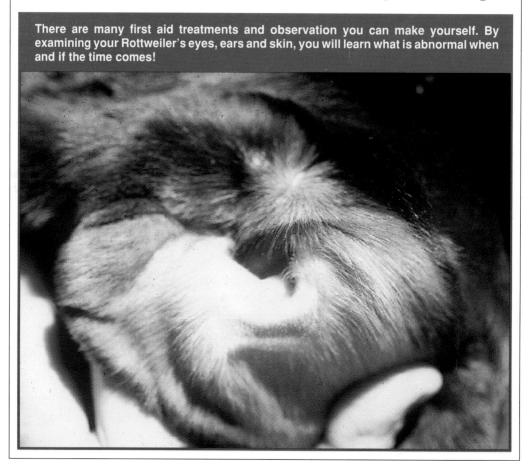

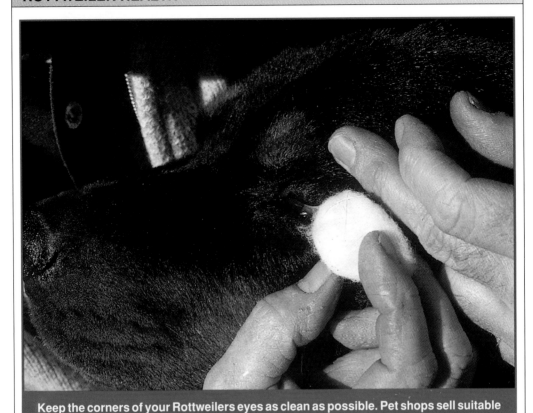

Keep the corners of your Rottweilers eyes as clean as possible. Pet shops sell suitable eye care preparations.

and you could get squirted if not careful. Veterinarians can take care of this during regular visits and demonstrate the cleanest method.

Many Rottweilers are predisposed to certain congenital and inherited abnormalities, such as hip dysplasia, a blatantly common problem in purebred dogs with few exceptions. Osteochondrosis and pancreatic disorders in Rottweilers are known, though not alarmingly widespread. The eyes can be prone to retinal dysplasia and entropion. Other problems, such as facial paralysis, epilepsy and hypothyroidism, affect some lines more commonly than others. Ask the breeder for records of any of

these problems before acquiring a puppy.

Hip dysplasia deserves special attention by Rottweiler people. As a result of the breed's enormous leap to popularity, more and more people are breeding Rottweilers, and too commonly with less than breeding-worthy stock. This congenital hip malformation can involve the absolute dislocation of the hip or simply a bad fit into the socket. The condition is present at birth but may take five to six months to a few years to manifest. All dogs should be x-rayed for the presence of hip dysplasia. Dogs who show bad hips should not be bred. The Rottweiler is designed to be a medium- large active dog: a Rottweiler who cannot run is hardly a Rottweiler. The ultimate effect of hip dysplasia is lameness. While heredity is critically involved in the occurrence of HD, environment should not be completely disregarded. Some breeders insist that one-week-old puppies, not given traction in their bedding materials, are more likely to develop HD than they would otherwise have been.

As with any large, deep-chested breed, bloat (also called gastric dilation-volvus or gastric torsion) is a life-threatening condition for the Rottweiler. GDV is caused by aerophagia, swallowing air that causes the stomach to be distended. Air gulping is a result of stress, vigorous exercise or bolting of food or water. Bloat implies that the flow of stomach fluid has been completly obstructed, resulting in the organ twisting. Bloat, if not treated immediately and vigorously by a veterinarian, results in shock, clotting abnormalities, heart problems and too often death.

Most breeders recommend that Rottweilers be fed three meals a day, and not one large one. Don't allow your Rottweiler to gulp his water and be very careful with overstressing the dog in strenuous exercise.

For the continued health of your dog, owners must attend to vaccinations regularly. Your

Never leave your puppies outside in the sun unless they have shade — better if they are removed to cooler areas after a short period of time.

Most of the ailments that affect Rottweilers are invisible microbes which can be treated if caught early enough. Contact your veterinarian as soon as your Rottweiler acts unusually.

veterinarian can recommend a vaccination schedule appropriate for your dog taking into consideration the factors of climate and geography. The basic vaccinations to protect your dog are: parvovirus, distemper, hepatitis, leptospirosis, adenovirus, parainfluenza, coronavirus, bordetella, tracheobronchitis (kennel cough), Lyme disease and rabies.

Parvovirus is a highly contagious, dog-specific disease, first recognized in 1978. Targeting the small intestine, parvo affects the stomach and diarrhea and vomiting (with blood) are clinical signs. Although the dog can pass the infection to other dogs within three days of infection, the initial signs, which include lethargy and depression, don't display themselves until four to seven days. When affecting puppies under four weeks of age, the heart muscle is frequently attacked. When the heart is affected, the puppies exhibit difficulty in breathing and experience crying and foaming at the nose and mouth.

Distemper, related to human measles, is an airborne virus that

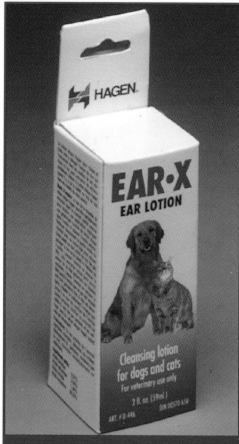

Keeping your Rottweiler's ears clean is simple if you use a top-quality lotion. It is essential that you maintain your dogs' ears, claws, mouth and fur. Photo courtesy of Hagen.

to 12 weeks. Older puppies (16 weeks and older) who are unvaccinated should receive no fewer than two vaccinations at three- to four-week intervals.

Hepatitis mainly affects the liver and is caused by canine adenovirus type I. Highly infectious, hepatitis often affects dogs nine to 12 months of age. Initially the virus localizes in the dog's tonsils and then disperses to the liver, kidney and eyes. Generally speaking the dog's immune system is capable of combating this virus. Canine infectious hepatitis affects dogs whose systems cannot fight off the adenovirus. Affected dogs have fever, abdominal pains, bruising on mucous membranes and gums, and experience coma and convulsions. Prevention of hepatitis exists only through vaccination at eight to ten weeks of age and then boosters three or four weeks later, then annually.

Leptospirosis is a bacterium-related disease, often spread by rodents. The organisms that spread leptospirosis enter through the mucous membrane and spread to the internal organs via the bloodstream. It can be passed through the dog's urine. Leptospirosis does not affect young dogs as consistently as the other viruses; it is reportedly regional in distribution and somewhat dependent on the immunostatus of the dog. Fever, inappetence, vomiting, dehydration, hemorrhage, kidney and eye disease can result in moderate cases.

Coronavirus is a type of

spreads in the blood and ultimately in the nervous system and epithelial tissues. Young dogs or dogs with weak immune systems can develop encephalomyelitis (brain disease) from the distemper infection. Such dogs experience seizures, general weakness and rigidity, as well as "hardpad". Since distemper is largely incurable, prevention through vaccination is vitally important. Puppies should be vaccinated at six to eight weeks of age, with boosters at ten digestive upset that is similar to, but much milder than, parvovirus infection. Once acquired by the affected dog, the virus spreads throughout the small intestine within four days. Symptoms include poor appetite, lethargy, vomiting, diarrhea, and dehydration. The digestive upset can persist or be intermittent for three to four weeks, after which most dogs will recover completely within seven to ten days. The main fear with this particular virus is the possibility of dehydration, which can be fatal. In this case, fluids are essential to replace the electrolytes lost. There is a vaccine available for this virus, and is typically given at six, nine, and 12 weeks of age. Other than administering the vaccine, the best way to avoid this potentially devastating disease is to keep the dog's environment clean. Because the virus is shed in the feces, dogs that are prone to coprophagia (eating feces) must be monitored in areas that are frequented by strange dogs, and daily cleaning of your Rottweiler's premises with a bleach and water solution is effective in deactivating coronavirus. Also, feeding your dog inside and keeping food safe from contamination by flies, roaches, and other insects will aid in decreasing the spread of the virus.

Parainfluenza is a virus that infects the respiratory system and combines with any of several other viruses to cause canine or kennel cough. Parainfluenza and other viruses spread rapidly, and the Rottweiler is particularly

susceptible. These types of viruses are very often contracted in large housing kennels where dogs are in close contact with each other, and therefore the disease is often referred to as "kennel cough." This disease can also be transmitted to and from cats.

Bordetella, called canine cough, causes a persistent hacking cough in dogs and is very contagious. Bordetella involves a virus and a bacteria: parainfluenza is the most common virus implicated; *Bordetella bronchiseptica*, the bacterium. Bronchitis and pneumonia result in less than 20 percent of the cases, and most dogs recover from the condition within a week to four weeks. Non-prescription medicines can help relieve the hacking cough, though nothing can cure the condition before it's run its course.

Keep this first aid cream on hand in cases of cuts as it is antiseptic. Photo courtesy of Hagen.

Keep a watchful eye on your dog for fleas and ticks as the open spaces is where they come from.

Vaccination cannot guarantee protection from canine cough, but it does ward off the most common virus that is responsible for the condition.

Lyme disease (also called borreliosis), although known for decades, was only first diagnosed in dogs in 1984. Lyme disease can affect cats, cattle, and horses, but especially people. In the US, the disease is transmitted by two ticks carrying the *Borrelia burgdorferi* organism: the deer tick (*Ixodes scapularis*) and the western black-legged tick (*Ixodes pacificus*), the latter primarily affects reptiles. In Europe,

Ixodes ricinus is responsible for spreading Lyme. The disease causes lameness, fever, joint swelling, inappetence, and lethargy. Removal of ticks from the dog's coat can help reduce the chances of Lyme, though not as much as avoiding heavily wooded areas where the dog is most likely to contract ticks. A vaccination is available, though it has not been proven to protect dogs from all strains of the organism that causes the disease.

Rabies is passed to dogs and people through wildlife: in North America, principally through the skunk, fox and raccoon; the bat is not the culprit it was once thought to be. Likewise, the common image of the rabid dog foaming at the mouth with every hair on end is unlikely the truest scenario. A rabid dog exhibits difficulty eating, salivates much and has spells of paralysis and awkwardness. Before a dog reaches this final state, it may experience anxiety, personality changes, irritability and more aggressiveness than is usual. Vaccinations are strongly recommended as affected dogs are too dangerous to manage and are commonly euthanized. Puppies are generally vaccinated at 12 weeks of age, and then annually. Although rabies is on the decline in the world community, tens of thousands of humans die each year from rabies-related incidents.

The undisputed champion of dog health books is Dr. Lowell Ackerman's encyclopedic work *Owner's Guide to DOG HEALTH.* It covers every subject that any dog owner might need. It actually is a complete veterinarian's handbook in simple, easy-to-understand language.

You need easy-to-clean food bowls for your Rottweiler puppy. If you get small ones, the puppy will soon outgrow them. If you get large ones, the Rottweiler puppy climbs into them. Which should you get? The large one because it can easily be cleaned between meals (which it should have been anyway!).

FEEDING

Now let's talk about feeding your Rottweiler, a subject so simple that it's amazing there is so much nonsense and misunderstanding about it. Is it expensive to feed a Rottweiler? No, it is not! You can feed your Rottweiler economically and keep him in perfect shape the year round, or you can feed him expensively. He'll thrive either way, and let's see why this is true.

First of all, remember a Rottweiler is a dog. Dogs do not have a high degree of selectivity in their food, and unless you spoil them with great variety (and possibly turn them into poor,"picky" eaters) they will eat almost anything that they become accustomed to. Many dogs flatly refuse to eat nice, fresh beef. They pick around it and eat everything else. But meat—bah! Why? They aren't accustomed to it! They'd eat rabbit fast enough, but they refuse beef because they aren't used to it.

VARIETY NOT NECESSARY

A good general rule of thumb is forget all human preferences and don't give a thought to variety. Choose the right diet for your Rottweiler and feed it to him day after day, year after year, winter

Dogs are not humans. Your Rottweiler does not require a constantly changing diet. Dogs do not have a high degree of selectivity in their diets.

and summer. But what is the right diet?

Hundreds of thousands of dollars have been spent in canine nutrition research. The results are pretty conclusive, so you needn't go into a lot of experimenting with trials of this and that every other week. Research has proven just what your dog needs to eat and to keep healthy.

DOG FOOD

There are almost as many right diets as there are dog experts, but the basic diet most often recommended is one that consists of a dry food, either meal or kibble form. There are several of these of excellent quality, manufactured by reliable concerns, research tested, and nationally advertised. They are inexpensive, highly satisfactory, and easily available in stores everywhere in containers of five to 50 pounds. Larger amounts cost less per pound, usually.

If you have a choice of brands, it is usually safer to choose the better known one; but even so, carefully read the analysis on the package. Do not choose any food in which the protein level is less than 25 percent, and be sure that this protein comes from both animal and vegetable sources. The good dog foods have meat meal, fish meal, liver, and such, plus protein from alfalfa and soybeans, as well

> **There are as many right diets as there are dog experts...the one most often recommended is kibble.**

as some dried-milk product. Note the vitamin content carefully. See that they are all there in good proportions; and be especially certain that the food contains properly high levels of vitamins A and D, two of the most perishable and important ones. Note the B-complex level, but don't worry about carbohydrate and mineral levels. These substances are plentiful and cheap and not likely to be lacking in a good brand.

The advice given for how to choose a dry food also applies to moist or canned types of dog foods, if you decide to feed one of these.

Having chosen a really good food, feed it to your Rottweiler as the manufacturer directs. And once you've started, stick to it. Never change if you can possibly help it. A switch from one meal or kibble-type food can usually be made without too much upset; however, a change will almost invariably give you (and your Rottweiler) some trouble.

WHEN SUPPLEMENTS ARE NEEDED

Now what about supplements of various kinds, mineral and vitamin, or the various oils? They are all okay to add to your Rottweiler's food. However, if you are feeding your Rottweiler a correct diet, and this is easy to do,

Select the best dog food and stick with it. Pet shops sell better dog foods than supermarkets because they care more about your dog.

All dogs need to chew...but only on substances which are healthy and safe. Unfortunately MOST dog toys are dangerous. Veterinarians only recommend Nylabone chew devices because they are the safest. Nylabone products are available from pet shops or veterinarians. If your dog doesn't chew on suitable products, it will lose its teeth. Rottweilers are especially in danger of poorly made dog toys because their jaws are so strong.

no supplements are necessary unless your Rottweiler has been improperly fed, has been sick, or is having puppies. Vitamins and minerals are naturally present in all the foods; and to ensure against any loss through processing, they are added in concentrated form to the dog food you use. Except on the advice of your veterinarian, extra and added amounts of vitamins can prove harmful to your Rottweiler! The same risk goes with minerals.

FEEDING SCHEDULE

When and how much food to give your Rottweiler? As to when (except in the instance of puppies), suit yourself. You may feed two meals per day or the same amount in one single feeding, either morning or night. As to how to prepare the food and how much to give, it is generally best to follow the directions on the food package. Your own Rottweiler may want a little more or a little less.

Fresh, cool water should always be available to your Rottweiler. This is important to good health throughout his lifetime.

ALL ROTTWEILERS NEED TO CHEW

Puppies and young Rottweilers need something with resistance to chew on while their teeth and jaws are developing—for cutting the puppy teeth, to induce growth of the permanent teeth under the puppy teeth, to assist in getting rid

of the puppy teeth at the proper time, to help the permanent teeth through the gums, to ensure normal jaw development, and to settle the permanent teeth solidly in the jaws.

The adult Rottweiler's desire to chew stems from the instinct for tooth cleaning, gum massage, and jaw exercise—plus the need for an outlet for periodic doggie tensions.

This is why dogs, especially puppies and young dogs, will often destroy property worth hundreds of dollars when their chewing instinct is not diverted from their owner's possessions. And this is why you should provide your Rottweiler with something to chew—something that has the necessary functional qualities, is desirable from the Rottweiler's viewpoint, and is safe for him.

It is very important that your

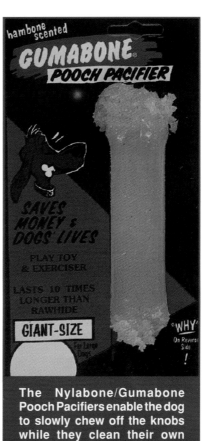

The Nylabone/Gumabone Pooch Pacifiers enable the dog to slowly chew off the knobs while they clean their own teeth. The knobs develop elastic frays which act as a toothbrush. These pacifiers are extremely effective as detailed scientific studies have shown.

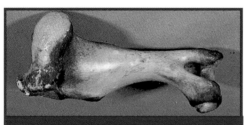

Pet shops sell real bones which have been colored, cooked, dyed or served natural. Some of the bones are huge, but they usually are easily destroyed by Rottweilers and become very dangerous.

Rottweiler not be permitted to chew on anything he can break or on any indigestible thing from which he can bite sizable chunks. Sharp pieces, such as from a bone which can be broken by a dog, may pierce the intestinal wall and kill. Indigestible things that can be bitten off in chunks, such as from shoes or rubber or plastic toys, may cause an intestinal stoppage (if not regurgitated) and bring painful death, unless surgery is promptly performed.

Strong natural bones, such as 4- to 8-inch lengths of round shin bone from mature beef—either the kind you can get from a butcher or one of the variety available commercially in pet stores—may serve your Rottweiler's teething needs if his mouth is large enough to handle them effectively. You may

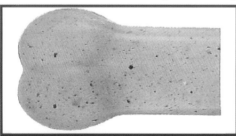

A chicken-flavored Gumabone has tiny particles of chicken powder embedded in it to keep the Rottweiler interested.

be tempted to give your Rottweiler puppy a smaller bone and he may not be able to break it when you do, but puppies grow rapidly and the power of their jaws constantly increases until maturity. This means that a growing Rottweiler may break one of the smaller bones at any time, swallow the pieces, and die painfully before you realize what is wrong.

All hard natural bones are very abrasive. If your Rottweiler is an avid chewer, natural bones may wear away his teeth prematurely; hence, they then should be taken away from your dog when the teething purposes have been served. The badly worn, and usually painful, teeth of many mature dogs can be traced to excessive chewing on natural bones.

Contrary to popular belief, knuckle bones that can be chewed

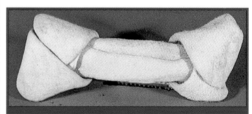

Rawhide is probably the best-selling dog chew. It can be dangerous and cause a dog to choke on it as it swells when wet. A molded, melted rawhide mixed with casein is available (though always scarce). This is the only suitable rawhide for Rottweilers.

up and swallowed by your Rottweiler provide little, if any, usable calcium or other nutriment. They do, however, disturb the digestion of most dogs and cause them to vomit the nourishing food they need.

Dried rawhide products of various types, shapes, sizes, and prices are available on the market and have become quite popular.

However, they don't serve the primary chewing functions very well; they are a bit messy when wet from mouthing, and most Rottweilers chew them up rather rapidly—but they have been considered safe for dogs until recently. Now, more and more incidents of death, and near death, by strangulation have been reported to be the results of partially swallowed chunks of rawhide swelling in the throat. More recently, some veterinarians have been attributing cases of acute constipation to large pieces of incompletely digested rawhide in the intestine.

A new product, molded rawhide, is very safe. During the process, the rawhide is melted and then injection molded into the familiar dog shape. It is very hard and is eagerly accepted by Rottweilers. The melting process also sterilizes the rawhide. Don't confuse this with pressed rawhide, which is nothing more than small strips of

Chocolate Nylabone has a one micron thickness coat of chocolate under the skin of the nylon. When the Rottweiler chews it the white subsurface is exposed. This photo shows before and after chewing.

rawhide squeezed together.

The nylon bones, especially those with natural meat and bone fractions added, are probably the most complete, safe, and economical answer to the chewing need. Dogs cannot break them or bite off sizable chunks; hence, they are completely safe—and being longer lasting than other things offered for the purpose, they are economical.

Hard chewing raises little bristle-like projections on the surface of the nylon bones—to provide effective interim tooth cleaning and vigorous gum massage, much in the same way your toothbrush does it for you. The little projections are raked off and swallowed in the form of thin shavings, but the chemistry of the nylon is such that they break down in the stomach fluids and pass through without effect.

The toughness of the nylon provides the strong chewing resistance needed for important jaw exercise and effectively aids teething functions, but there is no tooth wear because nylon is non-abrasive. Being inert, nylon does

Pet shops sell dog treats which are healthy and nutritious. Cheese is added to chicken meal, rawhide and other high-protein feeds to be melted together and molded into hard chew devices or pacifiers. Don't waste your money on low-protein treats. If the protein content isn't at least 50%, pass it up!

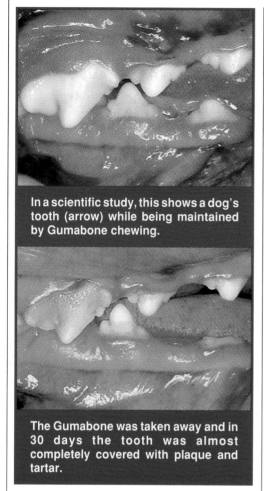

In a scientific study, this shows a dog's tooth (arrow) while being maintained by Gumabone chewing.

The Gumabone was taken away and in 30 days the tooth was almost completely covered with plaque and tartar.

not support the growth of microorganisms; and it can be washed in soap and water or it can be sterilized by boiling or in an autoclave.

Nylabone® is highly recommended by veterinarians as a safe, healthy nylon bone that can't splinter or chip. Nylabone® is frizzled by the dog's chewing action, creating a toothbrush-like surface that cleanses the teeth and massages the gums. Nylabone®, the only chew products made of flavor-impregnated solid nylon, are available in your local pet shop. Nylabone® is superior to the cheaper bones because it is made

of virgin nylon, which is the strongest and longest-lasting type of nylon available. The cheaper bones are made from recycled or re-ground nylon scraps, and have a tendency to break apart and split easily.

Nothing, however, substitutes for periodic professional attention for your Rottweiler's teeth and gums, not any more than your toothbrush can do that for you. Have your Rottweiler's teeth cleaned at least once a year by your veterinarian (twice a year is better) and he will be happier, healthier, and far more pleasant to live with.

The nylon tug toy is actually a dental floss. You grab one end and let your Rottweiler tug on the other as it slowly slips through his teeth since nylon is self-lubricating (slippery). Do NOT use cotton rope tug toys as cotton is organic and rots. It is also weak and easily loses strands which are indigestible should the dog swallow them.

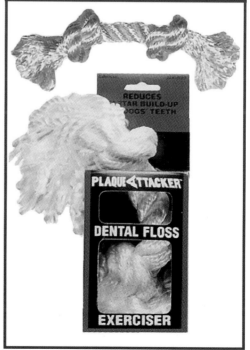

Most pet shops have complete walls dedicated to safe pacifiers.

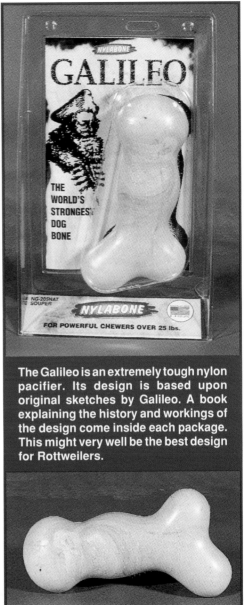

The Galileo is an extremely tough nylon pacifier. Its design is based upon original sketches by Galileo. A book explaining the history and workings of the design come inside each package. This might very well be the best design for Rottweilers.

Rottweilers have such strong jaws that most ordinary pacifiers (chew devices) are immediately destroyed. The Hercules has been designed with Rottweilers and other large breeds in mind. This bone is made of polyurethane, like car bumpers.

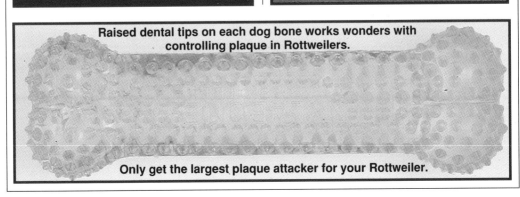

Raised dental tips on each dog bone works wonders with controlling plaque in Rottweilers.

Only get the largest plaque attacker for your Rottweiler.

All Rottweilers, puppies or adults, indoors or outdoors, must have clean drinking water available at all times.

TRAINING YOUR ROTTWEILER

You owe proper training to your Rottweiler. The right and privilege of being trained is his birthright; and whether your Rottweiler is going to be a handsome, well-mannered housedog and companion, a show dog, or whatever possible use he may be put to, the basic training is always the same—all must start with basic obedience, or what might be called "manner training."

Your Rottweiler must come instantly when called and obey the "Sit" or "Down" command just as chase cats, and he must be reprimanded for it.

PROFESSIONAL TRAINING

How do you go about this training? Well, it's a very simple procedure, pretty well standardized by now. First, if you can afford the extra expense, you may send your Rottweiler to a professional trainer, where in 30 to 60 days he will learn how to be a "good dog." If you enlist the services of a good professional trainer, follow his advice of when to come to see the dog. No, he won't

Only use Frisbees with a dog bone molded on the top. This shows the Frisbee was made for dogs and is safe for them to chew on (which they always do!). The bone also helps the dog get a grip on the Frisbee if it lands flat on a smooth surface.

fast; he must walk quietly at "Heel," whether on or off lead. He must be mannerly and polite wherever he goes; he must be polite to strangers on the street and in stores. He must be mannerly in the presence of other dogs. He must not bark at children on roller skates, motorcycles, or other domestic animals. And he must be restrained from chasing cats. It is not a dog's inalienable right to forget you, but too-frequent visits at the wrong time may slow down his training progress. And using a "pro" trainer means that you will have to go for some training, too, after the trainer feels your Rottweiler is ready to go home. You will have to learn how your Rottweiler works, just what to expect of him and how to use what the dog has learned after he is home.

In the photos above and below you can observe a Rottweiler being trained to SIT and DOWN with hand and voice commands.

The Frisbee for dogs can be used as a water dish,too!

Initial training is always with the lead; when the Rottweiler's education is more complete and dependable, you can train him without a lead.

OBEDIENCE TRAINING CLASS

Another way to train your Rottweiler (many experienced Rottweiler people think this is the best) is to join an obedience training class right in your own community. There is such a group in nearly every community nowadays. Here you will be working with a group of people who are also just starting out. You will actually be training your own dog, since all work is done under the direction of a head trainer who will make suggestions to you and also tell you when and how to correct your Rottweiler's errors. Then, too, working with such a group, your Rottweiler will learn to get along with other dogs. And, what is more important, he will learn to do exactly what he is told to do, no matter how much confusion there is around him or how great the temptation is to go his own way.

Write to your national kennel club for the location of a training club or class in your locality. Sign up. Go to it regularly—every session! Go early and leave late! Both you and your Rottweiler will benefit tremendously.

TRAIN HIM BY THE BOOK

The third way of training your Rottweiler is by the book. Yes, you can do it this way and do a good job of it too. If you can read and if you're smarter than the dog, you'll do a good job. But in using the book method, select a book, buy it, study it carefully; then study it some more, until the procedures are almost second nature to you. Then start your training. But stay with the book and its advice and exercises. Don't start in and then make up a few rules of your own. If you don't follow the book, you'll get into jams you can't get out of by yourself. If after a few hours of short training sessions your Rottweiler is still not working as he should, get back to the book for a study session, because it's your fault, not the dog's! The procedures of dog training have been so well systemized that it must be your fault, since literally thousands of fine Rottweilers have been trained by the book.

After your Rottweiler is "letter perfect" under all conditions, then, if you wish, go on to advanced training and trick work.

Your Rottweiler will love his obedience training, and you'll burst with pride at the finished product! Your Rottweiler will enjoy life even more, and you'll enjoy your Rottweiler more. And remember— you *owe good training to your Rottweiler.*

SUCCESSFUL DOG TRAINING is one of the better dog training books by Hollywood dog trainer Michael Kamer, who trains dogs for movie stars.

This magnificent Rottweiler is posing on command. This is the ultimate in show training and captures the hearts of most Rottweiler judges.

Rottweilers lined up and ready to compete and obey their master's commands. Rottweilers are large animals. They MUST be trained.

Pet shops sell doors through which your Rottweiler can enter and leave your house without you having to open/close a door.

YOUR ROTTWEILER PUPPY

SELECTION

When you do pick out a Rottweiler puppy as a pet, don't be hasty; the longer you study puppies, the better you will understand them. Make it your transcendent concern to select only one that radiates good health and spirit and is lively on his feet, whose eyes are bright, whose coat shines, and who comes forward eagerly to make and to cultivate your acquaintance. Don't fall for any shy little darling that wants to retreat to his bed or his box, or plays coy behind other puppies or people, or hides his head under your arm or jacket appealing to your protective instinct. *Pick the Rottweiler puppy who forthrightly picks you! The feeling of attraction should be mutual!*

DOCUMENTS

Now, a little paper work is in order. When you purchase a purebred Rottweiler puppy, you should receive a transfer of ownership, registration material, and other "papers" (a list of the

Don't select your Rottweiler puppy...let the puppy select you. The first Rottweiler puppy that comes to you is the one to buy.

This Rottweiler puppy is saying *TAKE ME HOME*. Can you mistake this *love at first sight*?

immunization shots, if any, the puppy may have been given; a note on whether or not the puppy has been wormed; a diet and feeding schedule to which the puppy is accustomed) and you are welcomed as a fellow owner to a long, pleasant association with a most lovable pet, and more (news)paper work.

puppies. True, you will run into many conflicting opinions, but at least you will not be starting "blind." Read, study, digest. Talk over your plans with your veterinarian, other "Rottweiler people," and the seller of your Rottweiler puppy.

When you get your Rottweiler puppy, you will find that your

There are two types of Rottweiler puppies: The ones preferring the company of another puppy and the one looking for a human as his pal. Maybe you need two puppies if you don't have time to be with your Rottweiler.

GENERAL PREPARATION

You have chosen to own a particular Rottweiler puppy. You have chosen it very carefully over all other breeds and all other puppies. So before you ever get that Rottweiler puppy home, you will have prepared for its arrival by reading everything you can get your hands on having to do with the management of Rottweilers and

reading and study are far from finished. You've just scratched the surface in your plan to provide the greatest possible comfort and health for your Rottweiler; and, by the same token, you do want to assure yourself of the greatest possible enjoyment of this wonderful creature. You must be ready for this puppy mentally as well as in the physical requirements.

TRANSPORTATION

If you take the puppy home by car, protect him from drafts, particularly in cold weather. Wrapped in a towel and carried in the arms or lap of a passenger, the Rottweiler puppy will usually make the trip without mishap. If the pup starts to drool and to squirm, stop the car for a few minutes.

small "package" to be making a complete change of surroundings and company, and he needs frequent rest and refreshment to renew his vitality.

THE FIRST DAY AND NIGHT

When your Rottweiler puppy arrives in your home, put him down on the floor and don't pick

When you take your Rottweiler puppy home keep in mind that everything in your home is strange and unfamiliar to him. Give the puppy a few days to acclimate to the new surroundings before you start training.

Have newspapers handy in case of car-sickness. A covered carton lined with newspapers provides protection for puppy and car, if you are driving alone. Avoid excitement and unnecessary handling of the puppy on arrival. A Rottweiler puppy is a very

him up again, except when it is absolutely necessary. He is a dog, a real dog, and must not be lugged around like a rag doll. Handle him as little as possible, and permit no one to pick him up and baby him. To repeat, *put your Rottweiler puppy on the*

As your puppy grows, he should be trained not to uproot your flower beds. Training of every Rottweiler puppy is mandatory. You won't be happy with an untrained Rottweiler.

There's a lot to be said for buying two Rottweiler puppies at the same time, but keep in mind that they both require feeding, training and vet fees. If you can afford it, go for it. Truly two puppies is three times as much fun as one puppy.

floor or the ground and let him stay there except when it may be necessary to do otherwise.

Quite possibly your Rottweiler puppy will be afraid for a while in his new surroundings, without his mother and littermates. Comfort him and reassure him, but don't console few minutes while you and everyone else concerned sit quietly or go about your routine business. Let the puppy come back to you.

Playmates may cause an immediate problem if the new Rottweiler puppy is to be greeted by children or other pets. If not,

The Rottweiler puppy in his new home requires understanding but not cajoling. Puppies are often afraid of the dark if you leave them alone. Try everything to make the puppy feel welcome during its first few days.

him. Don't give him the "oh-you-poor-itsy-bitsy-puppy" treatment. Be clam, friendly, and reassuring. Encourage him to walk around and sniff over his new home. If it's dark, put on the lights. Let him roam for a you can skip this subject. The natural affinity between puppies and children calls for some supervision until a live-and-let-live relationship is established. This applies particularly to a Christmas puppy, when there is more excitement than usual and more chance for a puppy to swallow something upsetting. It is a better plan to welcome the puppy several days before or after the holiday week. Like a baby, your Rottweiler puppy needs much rest and should not be over-handled. Once a child realizes that a puppy has "feelings" similar to his own, and can readily be hurt or injured, the opportunities for play and responsibilities provide exercise and training for both.

For his first night with you, he should be put where he is to sleep every night—say in the kitchen, since its floor can usually be easily cleaned. Let

Retractable leashes are the preferred type for Rottweiler. The Trakt enables you to adjust the length of the leash.

TRAKT RETRACTABLE LEASHES STOP & LOCK

him explore the kitchen to his heart's content; close doors to confine him there. Prepare his food and feed him lightly the first night. Give him a pan with some water in it—not a lot, since most puppies will try to drink the whole pan dry. Give him an old coat or shirt to lie on. Since a coat or shirt will be strong in human scent, he will pick it out to lie on, thus furthering his feeling of security in the room where he has just been fed.

HOUSEBREAKING HELPS

Now, sooner or later—mostly sooner—your new Rottweiler puppy is going to "puddle" on the floor. First take a newspaper and lay it on the puddle until the urine is soaked up onto the paper. *Save this paper.* Now take a cloth with soap and water, wipe up the floor and dry it well. Then take the wet paper and place it on a fairly large square of newspapers in a convenient corner. When cleaning up, always keep a piece of wet paper on top of the others. Every time he wants to "squat," he will seek out this spot and use the papers. (This routine is rarely necessary for more than three days.) Now leave your Rottweiler puppy for the night. Quite probably he will cry and howl a bit; some are more stubborn than others on this matter. But let him stay alone for the night. This may seem harsh treatment, but it is the best procedure in the long run. Just let him cry; he will weary of it sooner or later.

SUGGESTED READING

The following books are all published by T.F.H. Publications and are recommended to you for additional information:

Successful Dog Training by Michael Kamer (TS-205) contains the latest training methods used by professional dog trainers. Author and Hollywood dog trainer Michael Kamer is one of the most renowned trainers in the country, having trained both stunt dogs for movies and house pets for movie stars such as Frank Sinatra, Barbara Streisand, Arnold Schwarzenegger, Sylvester Stallone, and countless others. The most modern techniques of training are presented step-by-step and illustrated with fantastic full-color photography. Whether you are a longtime obedience trainer or a new dog owner, *Successful Dog Training* will prove an invaluable tool in developing or improving your own training skills.

Everybody Can Train Their Own Dog by Angela White (TW-113) is a fabulous reference guide for all dog owners. This well-written, easy-to-understand book covers all training topics in alphabetical order for instant location. In addition to teaching, this book provides problem solving and problem prevention techniques that are fundamental to training. All teaching methods are based on motivation and kindness, which bring out the best of a dog's natural ability and instinct.

Owner's Guide to Dog Health by Lowell Ackerman, D.V.M. (TS-214) is the most comprehensive volume on dog health available today. Internationally respected veterinarian Dr. Lowell Ackerman examines in full detail the signs of illness and disease, diagnosis, treatment and therapy options as well as preventative measures, all in simple terms that are easy for the reader to understand. Hundreds of color photographs and illustrations throughout the text help explain the latest procedures and technological advances in all areas of canine care, including nutrition, skin and haircoat care, vaccinations, and more. *Owner's Guide to Dog Health* is an absolute must for those who sincerely care about the health of their dog.

Dog Breeding for Professionals by Dr. Herbert Richards (H-969) is a straightforward discussion of how to breed dogs of various sizes and how to care for newborn puppies. The many aspects of breeding (including possible problems and practical solutions) are covered in great detail. *Warning: the explicit photos of canine sexual activities may offend some readers.*

In addition to the foregoing, the following individual breed books of interest to readers of this book are available at pet shops and books stores.

The Professional's Book of Rottweilers by Anna Katherine Nicholas (TS-147) is the most comprehensive volume on the breed available. Every possible aspect of the Rottweiler is covered in detail, from showing to breeding to the full-fledged working dogs that are performing around the world. In addition to the immense amount of information, *The Professional's Book of Rottweilers* is a fabulous collection of over 700 full-color photos of champion Rottweilers. Author Anna Katherine Nicholas is without a doubt the most prominent American authority on the breed, and she has presented a wealth of knowledge that is designed to be of interest to both the newcomer and the experienced fancier.

The Proper Care of Rottweilers by Joan Klem and Susan Rademacher (TW-142) covers all of the basics of Rottweiler ownership and care. From puppyhood through adulthood, this handy guide gives the Rottweiler owner all the details necessary for keeping your dog healthy and vibrant. Plus, to give the new owner an idea of what their Rottie should look like, it's illustrated with over 200 full-color photos of top-notch breed representatives. The authors, who are two of the most respected judges, breeders, and exhibitors in the fancy, provide valuable insight and a personal perspective on the breed that no Rottweiler owner should be without.

The New Rottweiler by Jim Pettengell (TS-202) is an updated version of one of the most in-depth works ever published on the Rottweiler. Australian breed authority Jim Pettengell has completely covered the early history, bloodlines, breed standards, and practical aspects of the Rottweiler around the world. This new edition is filled with double the color photography of the original edition, producing a handsome volume that belongs on the bookshelf of every Rottweiler owner.

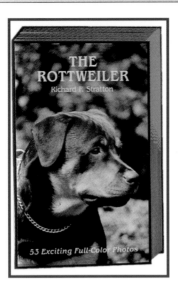

The Rottweiler by Richard Stratton (PS-820) details the practical uses of the multi-purpose Rottweiler. World-famous dog author Richard Stratton shares his knowledge gained from over forty years of experience with working dogs to present all of the facets of Rottweiler ownership. Whether you plan to show your Rottweiler, train for Schutzhund or obedience competition, use one as a guard/protection dog, or merely own a household pet, this book will give you all the specifics on care, management, and general husbandry. Entirely practical in its approach and

beautifully illustrated with color photography, The Rottweiler amply shows why this noble breed is so widely admired.

Breeding Rottweilers by Victoria Robertson (KW-229) is designed to guide the dedicated Rottweiler person to breed better dogs. The author-breeder has written a clear and concise account of the entire breeding process outlining sensible procedures, forewarning of the many complications and giving the reader a broad perspective of breeding to enable him to bring forth sounder Rottweilers. Illustrated throughout with handsome champion Rotties, this much-needed book intends to start the right people in their own successful breeding programs.

The Book of the Rottweiler by Anna Katherine Nicholas (H-1035) is for those dedicated Rottweiler owners and breeders who never get enough of seeing or learning about their breed. Anna Katherine Nicholas, a well-known judge for 50 years, has been in touch with most of the leading breeders in the country in order to research and obtain photos for this book, including those names that have been familiar in the breed for decades. For those experienced Rottweiler fanciers, this book will reinforce their knowledge of the breed. For novices, it will open a vast new dimension of owning/breeding/showing and provide an exhaustive reference book for sources and general information for years to come.

INDEX